Through the Blinds

By Amanda Clark

Copyright ©2012 Steady Moon Press

www.steadymoonpress.com
Woodsville, New Hampshire

ISBN-13: 978-0615648996
ISBN-10: 0615648991

Library of Congress Number: 2012941948

Printed in the United States of America

Dedicated as always, to my family, who support me in all I do,

and to Joel, who remains by my side.

Preface

I'll be honest, this book has been done for a while. Actually, it's been done for years. *Through the Blinds* was written in my early 20's, shortly after graduating college, and as I write this now, my 30th birthday waits around the corner. I wanted to get this book out sooner, but adulthood seemed to get in the way. I also admit, it just didn't feel right releasing it until now.

It's amazing how this is my fourth book. I have four chapters written of my life, and more awaiting to be released. Whenever I put out a book I am transported back in time. It's almost like reliving my past struggles and conquests. I am fortunate to hold words in my hands that explicitly detail my most important personal thoughts and memories. My books transport me back in time and allow me to relive the journeys that made me who I am today. *Through the Blinds* chronicles a voyage through stressful entry-level jobs, self-worth, independence, heartbreak, and redemption. Welcome to the next chapter....

Table of Contents

Come In

Come In, Come In
Come to me I say.

Offer your interpretation
        I'd like to hear.

I'd also like to show you mine,
if one does not mind.

A common audience
        that's all I want.
A tribute to the ordinary   No more stomping on the
"secondary."

No more fake and weary.

Makes me sick,
makes lullabies scary.

Also makes me WOUND AND ANGRY,
GROWN WITH FURY.

This compilation designates
The Every Man
The Every Woman

if you'd like to come in,
Come in-
You are invited   of course.

We gaze for reminders

of the past.
Recollections into the night.
Confused unity.
What causes this remote sadness
and interruption
from explosive happiness?

I want people who relate.
Take with you what you may,
        but please take away something.

That's all I ask,
        all I want,   all I hope.

If only you take away something,
it is then,

I shall be both satisfied and glad.

So come in
look around, ponder
and find.

I piece together many things

that many people may disagree with.

            I support my theories.

I go by time.
By instances.
Occurrences.

These things do not lie.

I may not understand how they relate
all I know is that they do.

I trust this notion.

I'll question it later,
as you will,

but I have few,
              if any doubts, at this moment.

That is all I know,
              I have no more answers.

Come in, I say,

              and read on...

The Thinker

Are we all just tortured souls

who revel into the night
and illustrate mad epiphanies

we ourselves cannot even fully comprehend?

My thoughts grow numb and distant
to far away lands

while my body resides here.

I expected a set plan.
A change of life.
A new experience.

It was lost to another.

One decision,

that is all it ever takes
to change the outcome
or living conditions.

One decision

that is all.

I imagined a future,
white chalk upon a blackboard,
a solid line,
a solution.

I felt confident and aware,
as if I had transcended or surpassed
a crucial time,
as if I had magically been able to take the
easy way out.

My confidence ran too strong
and because of this-
my
    mountain
        crumbled.

I picked my mangled body up
off the ground
    and sat upon
        the crumbling rocks and

                    rested my elbows on my knees

as if I was a marathon runner
drained of energy

and I sat there for a while
to gather my thoughts.

I sat there thinking about a solid black board, no
straight lines
or solid directions,

unpredictability hanging overhead,
smiling conveniently.

I remembered that
I was once taught that
the world is full of infinite possibilities.

Oh yes, it was that remembrance
that astounded me,
revived me,
and brought me back to my feet.

Logically, I could benefit more
Logically, I could make more
Logically, I could seek better opportunities,

but logic played a little role.

I will not say I am not scared
because that would be a lie through tightened teeth,

but neither will I say that I am over confident
because this displays a weakness too. I am somewhere
in the middle,
like the token monkey
at recess,

prancing back and forth

trying to catch that big red ball.

Thank You, Mr. Emerson

There comes a pivotal point
in most of our lives
when we decide that we
can make a difference.

It is a time
long awaited.

A time after hard work and recognition
of sacrifice.

It is a time when we finally stand up
and take a chance.

A time when we realize
that the greatest wealth
does not always include
gold coins and green paper.

A time when we learn that our small role
plays a significant role in others lives.

So many of us are scared of what we don't understand.
So many of us are hesitant to take leaps.
So many of us are blinded by the outside world.

I have held my darkness
and I have viewed sorrow.

Choose to sink or rise.

Figure out what makes you happy

and do it.

If you want to make a change

                        make it.

Hold hands with the misunderstood.

Bandage

I hold a pen with
a bandaged finger.

I cut my right index
on a metal sign.

Now it hurts to hold a pen.

Once again
the night has turned to morning
and I try to prevent the unwanted agenda.

We all must sacrifice to get to the top.
My sacrifice has become scarier
And more realistic
at the same time.

My days seem lost
and redundant,
I feel as if I am becoming closed minded

                        and a simple typical
figure.

I respect simple typical figures more because of this.

When I got home this evening
I parked my car,
got out, and lay down upon damp grass.

I lay there for a while as I gazed up at the endless
galaxies.

I decided I should do that more often,
I should find the time for such extravagant instances.
I should continue to revel in such significant far
away light.

Nothing hurt me as I lay there

I felt at peace,
this I remember, yes
how I felt at peace.

You probably want some wonderfully explained
revelation
or answer,

some political ideals or
philosophy on living.

I may not have what you are looking for.

      All I have is a description that
                       each one of us

     must figure out for ourselves.

Start

Embarked on a trip
　　　　　　　　not too far from home,

but far enough.

I wasn't really sure what I was looking for while
walking along cobblestones and cement, which
drew the heat to my body, while the sun
embodied me.

I could feel my skin tingling with red,
it was then, I realized, it had been a while since I had
retreated outside.

I pondered that day and gazed for something I loved.
Some place that would understand me and aid my
development.

I walked through a city and a country all in one day.

I began to piece together my life.
　　　　　I built a mountain out of spoonfuls of confidence.
Once again I began to believe.

This life is what we make of it.
There are choices that provide a world of limitless
possibilities

and there are choices that cause room
for the downfall.
　　　　　　　　Laziness tends to blend with the second.

Get up and do something! If you want to make a change
make it!

Put your actions where your words are!
         Make that difference!
Find something you love
and go for it!
Don't worry what others think, don't question, don't
sell yourself short!

Wake up one morning
         when the sky illuminates you from the
outside.
Wake up
And ask yourself,

what do I want?

It's not a difficult question really.
         What do I want?

If you have no idea
then get it together,

but if you do, even if it's a microscopic hint,
         well, it's then,
                           when you've found your start.

Who Names the Roads?

I fixed up my Camry.

Repaired the headlight I smashed against a truck
while backing out.

Repaired the mirror I took out on a telephone pole
while backing out.

This now hints to me, ever so silently,
that maybe, just maybe,

I should be just a little more careful
backing out.

Anyhow, I also got snow tires
and cleaned my car.
        Dusted, and vacuumed.
It feels different in there
as I drive.

Different, but good.
I like this.

I'm on my way back to the big ole' city
of Burlington, Vermont.
Actually, Burlington is hardly a city at all,
it's small and rural to me.

On my way I see one of those green signs
with the name of the place and the amount of miles
next to it:

Florence 3

and all I can think is, 'Isn't that magnificent,
I'm in the middle of Vermont and Florence is only 3
miles away.'

3 miles.

That's a universe.

Then I remembered my time in the real Florence;
an overwhelmed young woman
glancing in every direction at art,
white wine, cafés, umbrellas and laughter.

I didn't turn off
and follow the sign towards Florence,

I had a different agenda to follow.

I had commitments that no one could tear me from.
And so I passed that green Florence 3 sign
without hesitation.

I passed it and headed forward to my temporary home.

But for the rest of the ride
I could not help but wonder,
          who names the roads?

The Graduate

The graduate
submerges herself
in her backyard pool.

There's no breathing under water

but all the noise above
disappears.

Yes, underwater the graduate is able to find peace.

Above, *The Catcher in The Rye* lays on the deck, opened to the
very last page.

Above, through blurred vision,
she is able to see clouds wrestle with light.

It is then when she pictures
two circles of people,
      one chanting and dancing for rain and the other
chanting and dancing for the sun

and as she emerges from the cool blue water,
the graduate looks up at the sky

and shrugs her shoulders

because she finally accepts
                that

                      we need them both.

The Rest of Your Life

The rest of your life.

Catches one off guard
during a thunderstorm or during sunshine,
a reawakening
of our existing longings.

Who are you
and who do you want to be?
What did you picture
when you were young?

When does youth end?

I have seen and been a part of hard work

still, I do not represent its justice.

Yes, that deserves its separate line.

It's easy to sit back and say we all have the power to
Choose our passions
Live our dreams
Find our own missions.

These statements live a redundant clichéd life.

I may exaggerate, but I rarely lie.

I make real life into a story.

Bats

Who are these creatures
hovering into the night?
Like bats they are awake
like bats they are more productive
during the darkened hours.

A pile of classifieds
scatter on the floor
I still ponder and search for more.

More of this
more of that
            does it ever end?

Again I hover into the night
reading, writing, dreaming with opened eyes.

My imagery emerges through a lost soul
through an open mind
through a questioning existence.
My imagery describes me.

I am no imposter.
I repeat: no imposter am I.

This life I lead
I do decide.

Never under estimate
the genuine
Power of the mind.

Paper echoes from many places
read by many mysterious faces.

This is my genre.

I have been an athlete, an entertainer,
more credit emerged from such roles.
The independents struggle
the passionate must fight

and not surrender.

I cannot explain my formula

I do not scream weak nor strong
Nor right or wrong.

Respect my individuality.
Mingle together in harmony.

The night always turns back into day.

A poet's fate

                              becomes a bat's dismay.

Every

I'm back again with hidden lingo
back again with devout signals.
Try to distinguish between good and evil,
most of the time it is easy but sometimes there's an
upheaval.

I'm ready now
I'm happy now
I gave up a lot
and I'm still proud.

So question me another night,
tell me how to avoid the fight.
I'm calmer now
than I've been for a while
I'm confident and holding grace and style

I am no longer in denial.
I am no longer awaiting a fair trial.

What's art you say?
What will you do?
Sorry to say it, my friend,
but you have no clue.

I've rationalized the situation
I keep arriving to an obligation.

Someone keeps on singing to me in my sleep
a lullaby so beautiful
I sometimes weep.

I maintain I am going in another route
while memories show up that I had forgotten about,
with these I try to laugh out loud.

A new day to me always
delineates change
and some may think this is naive and strange
but don't you understand that I AM SOMEWHAT DERANGED!

Tell me what you want to hear
although it'll probably
pass through my ear.
I'll listen, but if I run away
don't cry with despair.
I do however charge for repairs.

And still I face questions
people always ask
maybe I should buy them a flask.

Where do your tales come from?
How do you think?

They don't realize that they are also in synch
and that's the problem
thought out loud.
That's the problem genuinely found.

I am no martyr, I am no saint,
I am no God I am no genius
I am no better
than any.

I've lost my rhyme.
I don't have to rhyme.

I've met people on mysterious paths.
Didn't remember if they were real or not.
Didn't remember them until morning.
Still I remember most of their stories.

Some say our lives are built out of a few essential
moments that determine our futures and existences

I say every moment is life changing

We just may not know it

at the time.

Keys

General of the Peloponnesian War, Aeschylus,
(as well as renown poet/playwright whom Sophocles sang
to when he was seven)
sat upon a rock one day with a glass of wine.

Overhead an eagle flying by
held a captured turtle
that fell from its claws
onto Aeschylus-

                killing him upon impact.
I stand reminded
of this fact, learned in Art History,
while under an illuminated Bank North sign
as I wait for the locksmith
to earn his 150 dollars
for letting me back into
my beat up Toyota Camry.

I lost my keys
somewhere between
this bank and CVS
not even 20 yards away.

Maybe they reside inside the store, I thought
so I scavenged
the aisles
searching particularly
where I recently bought three items:
a gallon of water, pretzels, and milk.

Searched for an hour

before I called the locksmith
who informed me of the one hundred and fifty dollars
I would be forking up.

I tell myself to think of it as the money I would have
paid toward
Mardi Gras
had I gone last weekend.

I also feel stupid for not having even one spare.

The silly efforts we make
to rationalize out absurdities.

The locksmith's Voxom van
displays 20 packs of Marb Reds on the dashboard,
that I counted soon after he arrived.

It also includes random scraps of paper
piled high and I wondered how he sees driving.

He smokes as he works,
as he tears the inside of
my door off,

and as I wonder,
is that really necessary?

He doesn't talk much
besides the three times he
asked me if I was sure that
my keys were not still in
my pocket.

The bank's located right before the highway at one of

the busiest
intersections I know of.
My area's magnified with street lights
that illuminate the whole situation
as if a Broadway play is taking place
inside the perimeter of this Bank North parking lot,

free admission to all.

I hear beeps every couple of minutes
from drivers flying by,
but I refuse to look up-
avoiding ridicule
for my random actions.

Such ridiculous
circumstances have led me here.

My rationalization
now makes
me laugh to myself,
'Wow,' I think,
'at least I didn't
get hit by a turtle.'

Burlington December

Scattered everywhere. So much that's new
So much left unexplained and unexpressed.
A series of events. A different way of learning.
Another challenge. Another twist of fate.

I have decided to tend to the children and people
Who are misunderstood and stigmatized.
I am now forced to hold in many secrets.

A responsibility and debt.

I cross the road from homes to playgrounds.

Patience holds a new definition, so does
responsibility.
So much has happened
And I am lost for words.

So far this week-a city was lost,
a heart pricked, a child left behind,
a special life
Stigmatized.

I distance myself,
I step in the middle.
I dance around with words.

I do my best to change a few lives for the better.
Donate what little money I have, work many hours for
more.

Earn little but do the things I enjoy, have desire

for, and believe in.

Divert the mind in other directions

while still maintaining a sense of
humor.

The Maze to Teaching

I was worried.
Awkward again, unfamiliar to my new surroundings.
Found myself traveling up one way streets.

I was frightened.
Now what? Everyone else was asking
so I began to as well.

I had seen too many aspiring greats
Empty their souls
and diminish
into specks of a life,

their piercing blue ecstatic eyes
Grew stale and dark. When I look into them now
all I see are sockets with entrance ways to black
holes.

No set plan captured my attention,
I merely had faith,
worked hard
and searched for
activities I loved.
Activities that I loved
and would not ruin me.

There were many days when I was unsure,
when persistence echoed but
I saw no source of the voice.

These days I sense a void
but I refused to immerse myself.

Persistence, patience, and pride
interlocked
and united to form my ultimate weapon
and my ultimate defense.

Finally, I have options
and choices.
The void began to fill
then overflow.

I sort through, weigh the options
file them as most beneficial and destructive.
I have learned that money
is not everything.
We need it, but I
can be happy off a modest living.
Off a modest living, I believe,
I shall be more rich than most.

I have never wanted to work in a cubicle,
to wear black loafers and have a mass produced desk
that I would sit at and look out the window all day,
that is if I was fortunate enough to have a window.
                              No thanks, corporate America.

I am not a fan of such a restricted work space.
I need variety day in and day out
if I wish to remain strong.

I am ready to join the force.
Not the army in war
but a hidden army of peace.

I am going to teach the children

because they are the only ones who
can end war.

If Any

I've seen a child
stand in the middle of a room
and sprinkle
cut outs of blue paper,
"It's raindrops," she said,
so casually,
I had to laugh.

I've seen a boy
with more knowledge than others give him credit for
argue that
the twin towers from September 11

were not forgotten
but the victims were.

I've experienced experiences I never would have known
if not for the life of a poem.

We underestimate
too much.
Most of us have egos.
We refuse to acknowledge and learn.
I believe we can all learn from each other.

We can all proceed.

Its not just a job to me
It's a solution.

Wander where you fear
it is then when you'll be closest to any answers

If there are in fact

Any answers at all.

Weather

The clouds continue to change.
A ghost warps into a fish,
a fish into a dragon, a dragon
into a new continent.

I feel like I am 10
again

                                                          with all the time

in the world

                and all of the freedom.

I should lay under the sky
more often.

The weather has been crazy lately,
dark and dreary with
lots of rain.
Today is the first day of sunshine
in an entire week.

I remain in my
backyard listening
to no-name bands

and trying to tan
while drinking
a screwdriver
in a healthy attempt.

I am engulfed in flames
on a beautiful day-

writing inside of a children's coloring book,
unused from when we were younger.

The cloud I was previously
looking at has traveled
Beyond my sight

Now a jet's trail
streaks across the sky.

How is it that I don't
miss anything

but all I look forward to
is a depart
away from familiar
land.

Such recycled phases.

Something's pulling me away,
calling me near.

I check to see if a string has been
tucked into my skin.

I hope to be led

into a field of
purple flowers and permanent sunny weather
and endless cloudy shapes.

I would stay there for eternity.

A Lot of Things

I was driving through
a town
I have not seen in
many years.

It once was the town
I saw everyday.

We grow to forget
much from the places we leave.

As I was driving, the sun
Disappeared
and an intense
rain storm appeared
to devour us all.

I could barely see
through my rain covered window
and had to pull over to the side.

Everyone who had been outside
was running inside,
everyone who was inside
remained.

Everyone,
except this one lonely girl,
this one girl who stared aimlessly forward.

She looked the same as anyone who would walk in the
sun.

It was as if she didn't
notice the flooding,

She had no umbrella, no jacket, she wore only a
soaking gray T-shirt and holey jeans.

I shivered looking at her
but she didn't seem to mind.

I wanted to know her story.
Was she lost?

Angry? Oblivious?
I would like to think she just
didn't give a damn about the rain.

I'd like to think she had no fear
and enjoyed the storm.

I'd like to think

a lot of things.

Welcome to the Next Phase

I'm sitting inside and I'm cold.
I've expected this time would come.
I expected and awaited the frost.
        Eagerness in other fields moved me here,
        and the cold doesn't bother me much at all.
I am floating where the current takes me
and enjoying the unpredictable outcomes.

I'm an older version of youth
learning more about the
"dignity of risk."

I am preparing to
live on a rocky shore,
one of beauty and
silence.
A rocky shore
that will no longer
cut my feet.

Here,
I feel safe, I feel free,
functional and at home.
Lessons and experiences
gained, I shovel them inside

while making footsteps in the snow.

The Noise Inside Us

When your words come,
use them,
they can be your defense, weapon and soul mate all in
one.
     Only a thin wall separates me from
   the outside annoyance

of midnight drunks
and passing cars.

Voices all around
but none are whispers anymore.

We all scream too much
and talk too loud.
   My voice seems to be vanishing
as I cough and sneeze and earn
a sore throat.

I listen more when I can't talk.
I hear things that I wouldn't hear otherwise.

Then I get bored, turn to paper
and my voice is back.
   I like how that works.

The noise outside does not bother me

   it's the noise inside, I use, to make a difference.

Code Words

What's going on in that head of yours?
It's easy to wonder
when in fact it's not much different
than wondering what goes on in this head of mine.
We looked at pictures of the Twin Towers today.
Tourist photographs of how they looked before.
Smiling faces with trademarks in the background.
Strange and haunting when
repeated.
There were pictures of after the storm
too, but those were skipped
quickly and without hesitation.
That was even more strange and haunting.
Illuminating a lost time,
framing life before their war,
ignoring the destruction.
A biased stance with an
understandable outlook.
My signed confidentiality
makes so much
difficult to describe.

Taking a Knee

Went outside to receive a breath of fresh air,
now I only feel sick.
What was meant to be a breath of fresh air only became
an asphyxiation
of lost desires.

I've had arguments lately over
tiny things
that amount to big problems.
Don't pretend you are better than me,
more superior because of a common language.

Don't compete
when there is no competition.

My stomach's churning
due to many reasons.

An imposter resides
where a good friend once stood.

I do not live perfectly,
but I vow to make mistakes.
Furthermore,
I am happy with not being in the lead.

Steps ahead
during relaxation
or racing to see a sunset
do not amount for me,
                                        they never will.

Do not correct me on lost causes.
I am not the same as I once was.
I will not stand for this incessant bullshit.
I'm blunt and honest
and proud.

Get it together.
We all have weaknesses

it is up to us recognize them
and fix them

      not project them upon others.

Through the Blinds

Through the blinds
I can see an old white Victorian house
with green speckled trim
and lots of windows.

On one sill a carton of orange juice, on another
a large plant, another a picture frame, another,   a
glass of wine.

Through the blinds
I can see fantasies,
I can make up stories, I can imagine fiction.

Through the blinds
I can build illusions:
brick by brick
stone by stone
nail by nail.

Through the blinds
I am an observer
of small ordinary worlds.
I am separate
longing and wishing.

Through the blinds
I am an outsider,
a lost soul
emptying and refilling ideal needs.

Through the blinds
I am partial,

darting my eyes
so I will see what I want to see
and using the blinds

to hide what I don't.

The Forgotten Ones

I'm sitting on my porch in my wooden
child-sized rocking chair
listening to music and writing.
Across the street a freshman dorm resides
and a few boys are kicking apples in the street
                           as cars roll by.
I am not amused.

I hardly ever look up
depriving them of their shallow attention.
Every once in a while I hear the clunk
of an apple hitting my steps,
I look up only once again to see them laughing
and slapping each other five
I look down quickly, unfazed,
pretending I hadn't even noticed.

They gave up soon after
                    or they may have just ran out of apples.

They had one of those small white bags with paper
handles,
the kind you get when you go apple picking.

I know because I went apple picking with my after-
school
children last week.

Some did not have the 2 dollar discounted price for a
bag
so my supervisor and I lent money to a few embarrassed kids.

When we are young (and some of us, when we are old)

unintentionally forget

about value.

Convictions

Why are there times
when we persecute our own convictions?

Convictions,
I think get us through many days
both rainy and hazy.

Convictions, I think make us view a brighter sun.
                    I walked to the waterfront
again this morning.
Hand guiding a mysterious source.

I am more prepared and calmer
than I once was.
        Predictions are preposterous to me now.
Convictions are still righteous.

Inside the "Insane" Mind

And so we meet again:
these crazy unstoppable mutual smiles.

I have been lifted up into the crowds
also though, I have been stomped
        and let down.
Stomped, and not asked about.

What if they are diagnosing the wrong ones as monsters?
Perhaps we "(the general public)" are the monsters.

We're all insane

and we don't even know it.

Every Human

Driving home
I had to laugh.
I thought, 'I lost a woman who only wandered outside
for a breath of fresh air and my car smells like puke,
and I am laughing because I feel complete,
useful, and joyful.
This is why I laugh
of course.'

Many times you just have to go with it,
hold a sense of humor
when others may want to run away.

I'm tired but I'm happy.
Stressed but alive.

I dangle foundations of oxymorons
and parables,
it's the only way anything makes sense.

I took an oath to not be too explicit
and this makes for an interesting way
                                of writing and conveying
that I did not have to face before.

A new challenge
I am prepared to deal with
and learn from.

I am able to embrace confidentiality and embrace

rights that should be available to every human.

5 Minutes

5 minutes.
What does it take?

Just scribble notes,
don't be lazy,
don't ignore.

I dressed up decently today-
            everyone wants to feel beautiful.
I made a few critical decisions.
I made a calendar of possible events. I released my
music.
I found my camera, I fixed my computer.

It's November 3rd again:
November 3rd, November 3rd....
I went outside this evening.
Clouds were all wispy
like stretched cotton.
They revealed a starry night.
Now I'm sitting in my favorite orange chair I saved
from the dumpster
with my bare feet against the cold wooden floor.

And I'm ecstatic really.

The coffee's steaming at 8:59 PM
and I am going to entertain myself into the night.

Never deny the muse, always get on the train
even if the train's already leaving
                        and one must leap.

There's been so many times when I thought I lost my
way,
now at such an unusual time
I've found it.
Not everything,   but something
and that's good enough for me right now. Yes,
that's good enough for me.

Five minutes-
          time's up.

Pure

She looks forward to her sunset outside
with hidden ashes behind a wooden pillar.

She does not wonder how many of her thoughts are pure
but recognizes that some
will ask.

This is why she steps outside.

One of the greatest compliments ever received
was from an older man
she had only seen once on a rainy evening in October.

He sat in the back of the audience and raised his
hand,
she called upon him
        and realized she had not noticed him there before.

"It sounds as if you are speaking to all of us,"
he said.
She nodded and shivered, "That's the point,"
was all she had to say.

It was the greatest compliment she had ever heard
regarding her passion.
She couldn't even express the importance,
the understanding, the thankfulness, the value, or the
        completeness
she felt then.

All she could do was go on to the next question.

And after the fulfilling event
she looked for the man
who had been sitting in the back row.

She looked everywhere
and all that remained
was an empty seat.

How strange, she thought.
He became an inspiration/recognition
of extraordinary motivation.

She wanted to thank him, that was all,
thank him for pointing out her life's work and goal.

She wanted to thank him for
explaining that all
was faithfully, emotionally, realistically,
                         pure.

The Stranger

I am prepared for another night without sleep.
Who needs it anyway?
I've wasted enough time.
I kicked off my shoes
shed my old school sweatshirt.
I've made my phone calls
I've attended my event.
I've drank my 6 pack.
I've watched my movie, read my book, listened to my
music.
I've looked out my window.
I've been outside.
I've filled out my applications and checked my email.
I've reviewed my poetry, gone for my walk.
I am searching for different words and different
themes.
Everyone's out of town.

I am a stranger to my own cause.

Last Night

I need to go for a walk
clear my head
seek my mood.

I want to leave without being recognized,
no name upon my back

I have formed a masterful disguise
a sweatshirt, long pants, a hood.

A face in the crowd of many
walking through a mad existence.

I kissed a loaded gun
last night.
I am leaving to escape the gun fire.

My Keyboard

I'd like to thank this keyboard
for putting up with my constant ramblings.
I convey my insides
and for this
I feel important
and righteous.
Now that's a strong word.
I am on free verse right now.
No stopping me now
who knows what this mind will spew.
You want to know
read on
although honestly,
I have no idea where I am going
or what I am about to announce or say.
Something got me started and so here I go
that's the only way my keyboard captures my undivided
attention
bet you haven't heard that phrase in a while.
What do you want me to say?
My mood's shifting.
My attitude's shifting.
My world's shifting.

Perhaps I create these moments.

They come so unexpectedly
mostly, I welcome them with a hinting gesture,
other times,
they appear uninvited
and I shiver and tense up
when I see them from across the room.

Energy is all around us
in all different forms,
energy rotates us, follows us, becomes us.

Energy provides us with light
and power, water, fuel
and memories.
                    Energy makes us or breaks us.

Tick-Tock

Is it a consistent ticking
announcing my time's demise
or is it
a steady drop of water trickling
                    from
                        some
                            unknown
                                source
                                    above?
Or it may be nothing more
than the switching on and off of the heater.

I was one of those annoying
participants this evening
who repeatedly **snuck**
glances at my watch.

I felt guilty each time
but I have to ask
why did the minutes
pause
without me?

Large

Small details, small details small details.
It pays to describe the things one thinks
may be so insignificant.

Those things, I've found, may be the most significant
of them all.

The saddest moments,
the tragic moments, the happy-
go-luck-trialed-moments.

The details,
the little details,

the way my grandmother's hand felt after the death
of her father,
cool and perspiring at the same exact time.

The yellow tulip I received from a lost
love so many years ago,

the way the moon looked,

the way the moon looked.

Far and whole and mysterious and smiling
with its concave craters.

My mother's red dress she wore while
dancing one evening with my father.

A Christmas gift wrapped in comic paper.

Or what about my stairway in Texas?
I used to sneak out my window and sit there for hours.
My fluffy leopard slippers resting on a cold metal
staircase.

The little details, the little details,

I do not think there's anything so incredibly
fascinating, ridiculously, intoxicating, or as
beautifully

LARGE.

Slam

A glass of wine
a glass of time
I want to slam or jam

whatever you "superiors" want me to call it.

I want to slip inside another night
I want to ignore the fight.

I need to find words that sound similar and true.
I need to see the truth in you.

Words echo and present a phase
are they real or constant haze?
Or are they a disgrace with a never ending maze?

The moon's on fire
the stars are still up
we all want to reach for the top.
Exploit that thought.

Expose who you are

                      and who you are not.

Figurines and Dragonflies

Begin with a wooden figurine and
a carved expression of
one holding the world.

I'd like to say pictures and phrases are screaming
from my head
but the truth is
that is not true.

The truth is I don't want to sound wonderful
and in tune
with perfect constructed melodies.

The truth is I stay at the apartment a lot
because I feel safe and productive
in my own little space.

The truth is I can be lazy.

Hours will go by and
I wonder what the heck I did all day
because I have a foggy recollection.

I enjoy retrieving the zone
but sometimes when
I find the space I
do not even know that I am there.

This can be exciting and scary-
like the snap of a finger.

My lamp looks like the leaning tower of Pisa,

slightly off balance, but somehow, still able to stand
up.
I make no effort to push it straight. Who cares?
I think it looks interesting and different and
stunningly poetic.
Plus the light shines where I want it to.

I feel powerful and alive
when I record a moment
because it's there in visual metaphors and allusion.

It's there so I can go back again
and try to understand.

It's as if I captured a speeding dragon fly
and kept it alive and
with me forever.

Concert

Mutual philosophies expressed in different art forms.
Blinking lights, strong voices.

I remember the times I listened
when all words seeped identical tunes of life.

When I understood backgrounds, experiences.

I understood much more than usual.

No one really knew You

                                                    when I was
introduced.

A gathering of love and devotion.
I can't describe all.

My view must have been different
than everyone else
but we still loved,
yes
        we still loved.
I remembered running, thinking, relating.
It was wonderful
and passionate.
I leaped and yelled,
moved and shouted.

Intoxicating to be around.

I didn't need anything more,
no other influence.

Nothing.

All was there,
all was perfect

all was mine.

It Just Is

You know those times when you don't
really know where the time has gone, when you haven't
anticipated a needed fall, or realized
exhaustion?

When the world has moved so fast without you and
there comes that critical unexpected time when
everything flies loose?

You lose it,

break down
even though you never saw it coming,

you freak out,
start crying,

cup your face in your hands

then,
once again
you become reborn to some extent
all over

and after, triumphantly,
you are complete, sane and almost,
yes, almost
            whole.

That's me. I'm that tornado
scavenging through the darkness
tearing down houses

and anything else that gets in my way.

I am no longer the peace before the storm.

I am a wrecking ball with
needed destruction.

I am the fear stuck inside innocent minds
who are running away.

I am the power to continue
and gain from my loss.

I am a lesson learned from depravity.

I needed a good run through the woods,
a good run in the pouring rain
where I felt drenched to the bone
and when I could scream myself into beautiful
oblivion.

That's what I needed,
and in my own little way
        that's what I got.

I have ignored one of my greatest passions and
therapies for too long
and for this
a building up so intense
        and long provoked
ate away like a broken heart.

There's no excuse really, I have never been fond of
excuses.

I deliberately knew what I did
even though it made little, if any,
sense at all.

I didn't really have an explanation
of my collaborated burdens
I only had my words and
shouts.

I had abandoned my paper
and because of this a streak of sanity was completely
and overwhelmingly

lost.

Was it an experiment?
A ridiculous trial?
Truth be told, I am not sure what it was.
                              A basin of undeniably wasted talent?

When do limits occur?
I used to shrug off small little details
when these are the details worth remembering.

There are limits. Set in our minds not stone
set in our humanity.

Yes, there are limits
and yes there are breaking points.

Do I sound redundant?
Redundancy, so I've been told,
is a reoccurring theme of mine
although it took thought out recognition for me to
understand or see the matter.

I have come to believe that there are essential times
for repeats.
       Now is one of them.

I explain myself with cycles and contradictions.
And that's it.   That's who I am.

It's not right nor wrong
            it just is.

The Wall

Pull my emotions out of me,
a few were hidden so deep
I didn't even know they were there.

I can hide little now.
I shouldn't be hiding anything at all.

Two souls so independent, yet intertwined.

And all this craziness in my head.
Have I lost my rationality
like I predicted?
Or have I gained logical destinations?

I have been confused many times before
but never like this.

This confusion parallels any other
because it's not black or dark
or light or clear-

I don't even know the color of this confusion.

It does not devour me or shadow
nor does it smile and greet.

And when I am apart
I feel   incomplete
as if I have been amputated.

This is wild crazy madness
I am not used to.

And one questions certain desires and motives and
expressions
when I tend to roll to the other side

and face the wall

because the wall cannot read my lips or eyes

the way You

can.

To Vacations and Fortunate Accidents

Vacations put so much into perspective.
We get worn down, exhausted,   bored.

Then if we are lucky, finally,
a vacation becomes possible,
or required.

I just got back from mine
and now I am ready to go back to work.
Ready to take on the craziness of my schedule,
the intensity of my chosen lifestyle.
                                        I even ordered a punching bag
today!

I am alive again.

I am also making some changes in the grinding system.
I am keeping old roots but trying out for different
roles.
I have become more organized, logical
and now I am thinking in terms of my own well-being.

I have many fortunate accidents
to thank.
Some, more than others,

One more than all.

Empty

So much is in my head
yet I find little to write about.
Every whispering thought

has some trace of You in it.

I try not to think of You

and then You only become more apparent.

Things are much different without You around.
I am not myself.

You're everywhere
and nowhere.

It's New Years Eve in Vermont.
It's black as space outside.
It's also snowing,
I can see the snow because of the street lights
it's snowing beautifully and silently
and romantically.
               And I feel

                                          Empty.

The Detour

The first day of the year has arrived
and I actually feel somewhat rested, alive
and don't have a stomach ache.
My eve consisted of piecing together a mystery jig-saw
puzzle
with a few tall glasses of white wine,

missing the ball drop with a lifelong friend, and
talking
to a long distance love into the early morning.

It wasn't anything too terribly exciting
but it was simple, it was good, and it was needed.

Today the snow is falling again and my hometown
radiates with a white winter land spectacle.
It's truly divine.

I decide to take a drive
and on this drive I saw the most magnificent
views.

The sky was misty gray
and above me there appeared to be a translucent hole
where a stark white full moon emerged.

I looked away for but an instant and when I looked
back
the sky had swallowed the moon, there was no trace
of the holy moment
all that was left was a blank limitless sky.

I kicked myself for not having my camera,
It would have been the most perfect picture.

Beauty shows itself in mysterious places
and often catches me by surprise.
                    Such is a prize for life.

I decided to take a detour to visit an old friend.

The graveyard road was slippery and narrow
but I made it through and parked in my usual spot.

It was hard to find him in the snow,
the names were covered on many stones.

I don't like walking in graveyards because I never
know where to step.

I always think that I wouldn't want someone stepping
on me, so I try to walk around them
but there are too
many spaces to avoid.

I found him quickly despite his covered name.
I wiped off the snow with my bare hand,
every part of it, the front the back, the top.
I crouched down and placed my hand on the cold stone.

I didn't say anything for a couple minutes
I just kept my hand on that stone with the snow
falling all around me.

"Happy New Years," I finally said, "we all miss you,
you are not forgotten."

It's been over six years.

I don't come here as often as I used to.

I've traveled away to various places and
I don't live around here anymore.

We've all grown up
and most of us have moved.

I heard once from a wise woman
that when you go to a cemetery to visit someone
the person you visit,
walks with you to the grave and
stands beside you
while you're there.

I believe that.

I can picture him standing there smiling, because
that's what he always did
appreciating the visit but also telling each and every
one of us that he is okay
and not to worry about him because he never liked
worrying that much either.

That drive through the snow
was unplanned and random.
For some reason I just wanted to go for a ride.

Life leads us to mysterious places,
we don't always see the meaning, many times we don't

but we still travel,
        and eventually arrive.

Real

It's foggy here in Southern Vermont.
The trees are naked and black
And ice seems to be everywhere.

All I can think of is You,
drinking tea
In a tropical land
before a hard days work.

I imagine that You are happy
because You are doing something,
no matter how hard the labor or difficult the task.

You hated being lazy.

It's been less than a week since You left.

Since I watched in steady silence as You packed up
Your last box.
Since You touched my face, ever so gently, on the way
to Your car.
Since You held me in your arms as I buried my face in
your chest.

I remember the smallest details about that day.
The way I stood by Your open window that same morning
and stared at a long white streak in the sky
left by a jet.
I remember I stared at it for so long
it disappeared right in front of me
and I didn't even notice until it was gone.

But most of all, I remember the time right before You left,
when I cried while kissing You
and all I could hear were wind chimes.
Yes the wind chimes, it sounded like there were hundreds of them
playing this chaotic melody
my ears could not decipher.

And it was also during this time
when I began to feel
incredibly lost-
as if my home
had burnt down

and nothing   was left   but ashes.

It was a feeling I had never had before.

And I remember driving away from You
thinking, so this is it, it radiates, it hurts, it
burns,

It's real.

Snow Pants

Today was the first day I had snow pants at my after
school program
where I work with 30-35 little kids.

What an experience.

They began by chasing me with snowballs

it was wonderful.

My highlight was creating snow angels.

They all gathered beside me
and fell like dominoes into the powder.

Now I'm home drinking a glass of my deserved red wine that has
a twist off
cork.

I am so thankful.

I have attended 5 hours of social work,
and spoken to the one of love.

A lot goes on within a day.

Some days resemble a life I suppose.

The Present

I've found many distractions,
by "distractions" I refer to my job,
my music, my walks, my cooking, my yoga, my cleaning,
my phone calls, my driving etc.

Things that normally would not be classified as
distractions at all.

I listen to more music now, I exercise more, I clean
more, I clap at more scheduled work hours.

I sleep in Your bed.

You gave it to me before You left-
my old bed had a spring broken and Your bed was
comfier You said,
            plus You had nowhere to put it.
Your Christmas present to me.

I am beginning to ask myself
If You were being polite and thoughtful

                                                    or

just incredibly cruel.

It's the first time I've ever questioned Your
intentions.

Forecast

The rain is streaking down main street-
I am
standing in the window
at 12:00 PM
in my bath robe
holding a cup
of coffee and
thinking of You-
      as usual.

Tomorrow I fly to You
                         rain, snow, sleet, sun
I fly to You.

And although I wish the hours away until then
I cannot help thinking about flying away from You
again.

It's a mind game, this love,
as we have come to call it.

          Drenching me with longing
                    and expanding my soul.

Will anything change after tomorrow
when I'm in Your arms again
breathing in Your intoxicating grin?
Will anything change at all?

And as I continue to gaze out into the rain
I wonder what the weather's like where You are?
Partly cloudy? Chance of showers?

Or absolutely

no

sign

of rain at all?

I Resign

Deep breaths.   Yoga.   A wailing of the punching
bag!
                                  A scream alone
in my car.

Tears exploding in my hands.

I am quitting a job today,
the first time I have ever quit anything really
and it makes sense,
it is right, and it is justified
        but it's still hard.

So much has been thrown at me
and I have dodged nothing.

I have stood there
and let myself be continuously shot.

I have to think of what's best for me.
I need to look at what I want to do
and impress myself this time
no one else.

I'm making a change
I am sacrificing many things
    but I am making a change.
I am going to get through this!
I am strong!
I am worthy!
I am passionate!
I am intelligent

and I am in love.

I am so many things
and I am going to look out for myself this time.
I am not going to combust,
but break away
and do what makes me happy
or what will inevitably
                    lead to
happiness.

Through the Blinds 2

Through the blinds
I see car headlights
a dark evening
and floating snow.

Through the blinds
I see
midnight drunks and
hear snappy high heels.

Through the blinds
I hear
hurtful whispers.

I like being inside
and not out within the blistering cold.
I am protected
here
even though no one else resides in my household.

Once again
this is not what I signed up for
but this is what I got.

I am missing You
more than ever.
I ache inside and out
all I want
is to touch Your face.
It's killing me
and I don't know how to avoid it.

These are my words of honesty.
I will make it through.

I have to.

I will
it's just harder than I ever thought.

I grimace at the months ahead
without You.

Get out of my head
how did You do this
why did You do this
what can I do to avoid this?

Through the blinds
there are whizzing cars and strangers
there are smashing bottles
of the homeless
in search for more.

Through the blinds there is so much
I cannot understand.
I wanted to release a little energy
so here I am
babbling about my mass confusion
and unpredictable irrationality.
I am aching inside
is the brutal honesty.

I am hurting because of You
and your clever words.

Your intoxicating rage
and intensifying charm.

I am aching from loneliness
and lust
I am contaminated with desire.

and the worst hurt of all
is thinking about the time
when I thought all was over
and You were not mine anymore
and me,
no longer Yours.
The contemplation of those words
twisted my stomach and
trickled like jagged knives
down my spine.

I am all out of sorts
and have little control.

So this is love.
The best never comes easy does it?
It hurts.
That's all I can do to describe it.
It hurts.
That's brutal intellectual honesty in simplicity

that's the truth.

We make things so much more difficult than they have
to be.

I want You, I need You, I love You
and I know You feel the same about me
but we stand here on other sides of the universe
twiddling our fingers and standing still

we are so stupid
and so afraid.

How long can this draining pain carry on?
How much can our love overcome?

Apollo and Dionysus are Watching

Everything became bleak,
the sky around me,
the trees all
bare,
exposed in their nakedness.

I wanted to numb my mind-
not think anything, not
let one single thought escape.

I wanted not to feel
anything at all.

I had never felt so weak,

or so alone.

And all around me
shadows fell,
clouds overcame,
the sun left.
So I went back inside,
locked the door, shut the blinds.

I walked to my mirror
and looked at my face,
red and full of so much hurt.

Then I looked into my own eyes

and through all the devastation

I saw a change
so relevant and pure and emotional

it was a change I had never seen before

it was a strength never to be reckoned with.

About the Author

Amanda Clark currently resides in Woodsville, New Hampshire. She teaches English and Social Studies at an alternative school in Bradford, VT. She is the author of three previous books of poetry, all of which she considers to be, "chapters of her life," including, *Looking at the Moon, Flying Fall,* and *Beautifully Mixed-Up World.* She was also a contributing poet for *The Litchfield Literary Review.*

Clark graduated with a Bachelor's degree in Art History from Southern Methodist University in Dallas, TX. She also graduated with a Master of Arts in Teaching degree from the University of Vermont in Burlington, VT. Additionally, she has studied abroad in Spain, Italy, and New Zealand. Her previous vocations include social work and outdoor education. Clark's poems have been distributed to classrooms, art galleries, libraries, and various newspapers. If you would like to contact Amanda, email her at: bigredac@yahoo.com
Her website is also available at:
https://sites.google.com/site/amandaclarkauthor/home

www.ingramcontent.com/pod-product-compliance
Lightning Source LLC
Chambersburg PA
CBHW071826020426
42331CB00007B/1625